Books with pictures by
Gyo Fujikawa

A CHILD'S GARDEN OF VERSES

THE NIGHT BEFORE CHRISTMAS

BABIES

BABY ANIMALS

MOTHER GOOSE

A CHILD'S BOOK OF POEMS

THIS BOOK BELONGS TO

A Child's Book of Poems

Pictures by

GYO FUJIKAWA

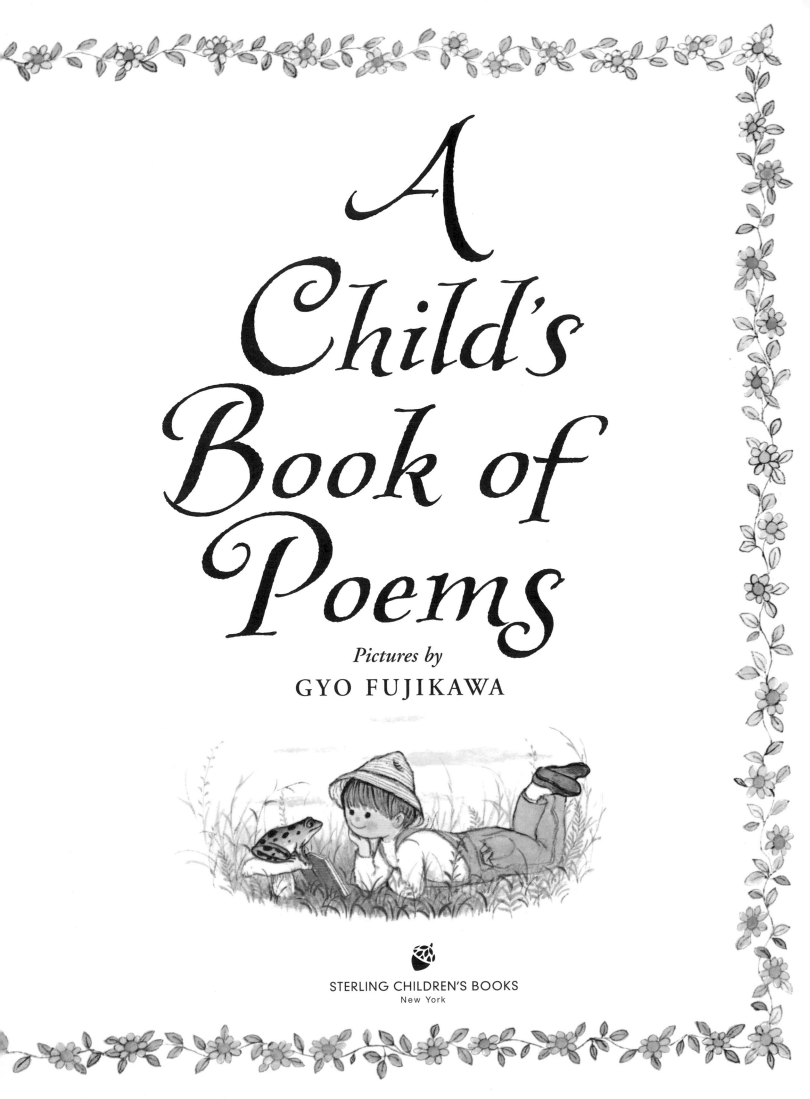

STERLING CHILDREN'S BOOKS
New York

STERLING CHILDREN'S BOOKS
New York

An Imprint of Sterling Publishing
387 Park Avenue South
New York, NY 10016

ISBN 978-1-4027-5061-8

Library of Congress Cataloging-in-Publication Data

A child's book of poems / illustrated by Gyo Fujikawa.
    p. cm.
Originally published: New York : by Grosset and Dunlap, [1969].
ISBN-13: 978-1-4027-5061-8
ISBN-10: 1-4027-5061-7
1. Children's poetry. 2. Poetry—Collections. I. Fujikawa, Gyo,

PN6109.97.F85 2007
808.810083—dc22
                    2007008211

Distributed in Canada by Sterling Publishing
c/o Canadian Manda Group, 165 Dufferin Street
Toronto, Ontario, Canada M6K 3H6
Distributed in the United Kingdom by GMC Distribution Services
Castle Place, 166 High Street, Lewes, East Sussex, England BN7 1XU
Distributed in Australia by Capricorn Link (Australia) Pty. Ltd.
P.O. Box 704, Windsor, NSW 2756, Australia

For information about custom editions, special sales, premium and corporate purchases, please contact
Sterling Special Sales Department at 800-805-5489 or specialsales@sterlingpublishing.com.

Manufactured in China
Lot #:
16 18 20 19 17
01/19

Contents

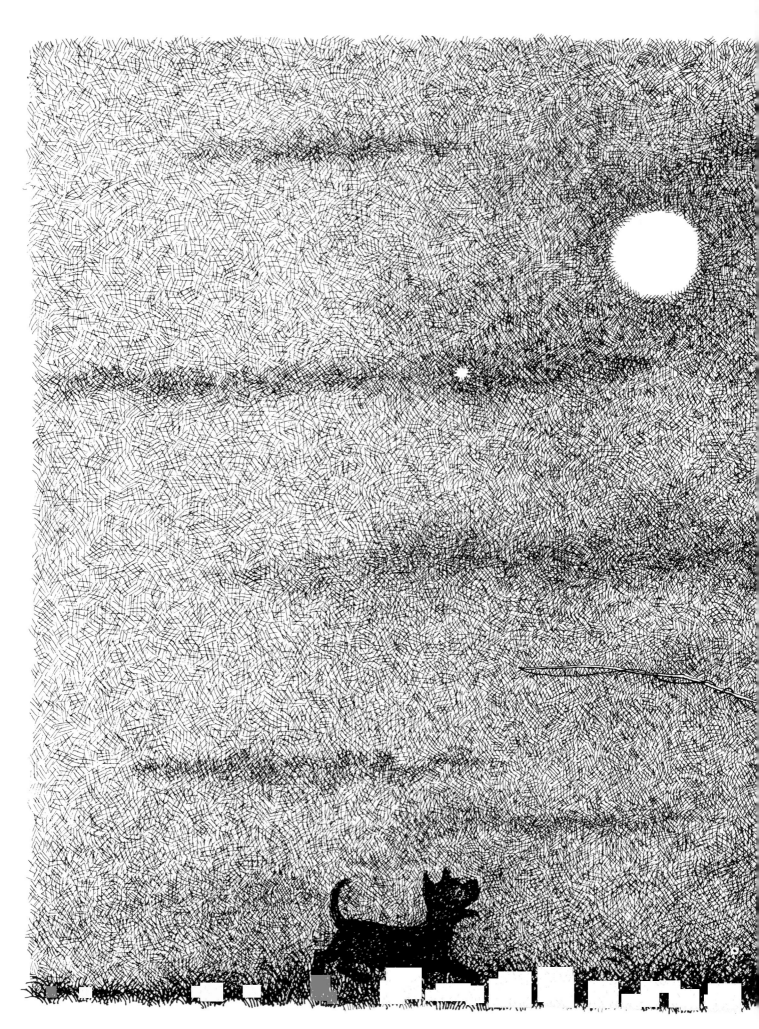

NIGHT

The sun descending in the west,
    The evening star does shine;
The birds are silent in their nest,
    And I must seek for mine.
The moon, like a flower,
In heaven's high bower,
With silent delight
Sits and smiles on the night.

Farewell, green fields and happy groves,
    Where flocks have took delight.
Where lambs have nibbled, silent moves
    The feet of angels bright;
Unseen they pour blessing,
And joy without ceasing,
On each bud and blossom,
And each sleeping bosom.

William Blake

WHICH IS THE WAY TO SOMEWHERE TOWN?

Which is the way to Somewhere Town?
　　Oh, up in the morning early;
Over the tiles and the chimney pots,
　　That is the way, quite clearly.

And which is the door to Somewhere Town?
　　Oh, up in the morning early;
The round red sun is the door to go through,
　　That is the way, quite clearly.

Kate Greenaway

SUMMER SUN

Great is the sun, and wide he goes
Through empty heaven without repose.
And in the blue and glowing days
More thick than rain he showers his rays.

Though closer still the blinds we pull
To keep the shady parlor cool,
Yet he will find a chink or two
To slip his golden fingers through.

The dusty attic spider-clad
He, through the keyhole, maketh glad;
And through the broken edge of tiles
Into the laddered hayloft smiles.

Meantime, his golden face around
He bares to all the garden ground,
And sheds a warm and glittering look
Among the ivy's inmost nook.

Above the hills, along the blue,
Round the bright air with footing true.
To please the child, to paint the rose,
The gardener of the world, he goes.

Robert Louis Stevenson

NESTING TIME

Wrens and robins in the hedge,
    Wrens and robins here and there;
Building, perching, pecking, fluttering,
    Everywhere!

Christina Rossetti

HURT NO LIVING THING

Hurt no living thing:
    Ladybird, nor butterfly,
Nor moth with dusty wing,
    Nor cricket chirping cheerily,
Nor grasshopper so light of leap,
    Nor dancing gnat, nor beetle fat,
Nor harmless worms that creep.

Christina Rossetti

THE CALL

Come, calf, now to mother,
Come, lamb, that I choose,
Come, cats, one and t'other,
With snowy-white shoes,
Come, gosling all yellow,
Come forth with your fellow,
Come, chickens so small,
Scarce walking at all,
Come, doves, that are mine now,
With feathers so fine now!
The grass is bedewed,
The sunlight renewed,
It's early, early, summer's advancing
But autumn soon comes a-dancing!

Bjornsterne Bjornson

BE LIKE THE BIRD

Be like the bird, who
Halting in his flight
On limb too slight
Feels it give way beneath him,
Yet sings,
Knowing he hath wings.

Victor Hugo

IN A CHILD'S ALBUM

Small service is true service while it lasts;
Of humblest friends, bright creature, scorn not one;
The daisy, by the shadow that it casts,
Protects the lingering dewdrop from the sun.

William Wordsworth

KINDNESS TO ANIMALS

Little children, never give
Pain to things that feel and live;
Let the gentle robin come
For the crumbs you save at home;
As his meat you throw along
He'll repay you with a song.
Never hurt the timid hare
Peeping from her green grass lair,
Let her come and sport and play
On the lawn at close of day.
The little lark goes soaring high
To the bright windows of the sky,
Singing as if 'twere always spring,
And fluttering on an untired wing —
Oh! let him sing his happy song,
Nor do these gentle creatures wrong.

WYNKEN, BLYNKEN, AND NOD

Wynken, Blynken, and Nod one night
    Sailed off in a wooden shoe —
Sailed on a river of crystal light,
    Into a sea of dew.
"Where are you going, and what do you wish?"
    The old moon asked the three.
"We have come to fish for the herring fish
    That live in this beautiful sea;
    Nets of silver and gold have we!"
        Said Wynken,
        Blynken,
        And Nod.

The old moon laughed and sang a song,
    As they rocked in the wooden shoe,
And the wind that sped them all night long
    Ruffled the waves of dew.
The little stars were the herring fish
    That lived in that beautiful sea —
"Now cast your nets wherever you wish —
    Never afeared are we";
    So cried the stars to the fishermen three:
        Wynken,
        Blynken,
        And Nod.

All night long their nets they threw
   To the stars in the twinkling foam —
Then down from the skies came the wooden shoe,
   Bringing the fishermen home;
'Twas all so pretty a sail it seemed
   As if it could not be,
And some folks thought 'twas a dream they'd dreamed
   Of sailing that beautiful sea —
   But I shall name you the fishermen three:
      Wynken,
      Blynken,
      And Nod.

Wynken and Blynken are two little eyes,
   And Nod is a little head,
And the wooden shoe that sailed the skies
   Is a wee one's trundle-bed.
So shut your eyes while mother sings
   Of wonderful sights that be,
And you shall see the beautiful things
   As you rock in the misty sea,
   Where the old shoe rocked the fishermen three:
      Wynken,
      Blynken,
      And Nod.

Eugene Field

THE SUGARPLUM TREE

Have you ever heard of the Sugarplum Tree?
    'Tis a marvel of great renown!
It blooms on the shore of the Lollipop Sea
    In the garden of Shut-eye Town;
The fruit that it bears is so wondrously sweet
    (As those who have tasted it say)
That good little children have only to eat
    Of that fruit to be happy next day.

When you've got to the tree, you would have
      a hard time
    To capture the fruit which I sing;
The tree is so tall that no person could climb
    To the boughs where the sugarplums
      swing!
But up in that tree sits a chocolate cat,
    And a gingerbread dog prowls below —
And this is the way you contrive to get at
    Those sugarplums tempting you so:

You say but the word to that gingerbread dog
    And he barks with such terrible zest
That the chocolate cat is at once all agog,
    As her swelling proportions attest.
And the chocolate cat goes cavorting around
    From this leafy limb unto that,
And the sugarplums tumble, of course, to the
      ground —
    Hurrah for that chocolate cat!

There are marshmallows, gumdrops, and
      peppermint canes,
    With stripings of scarlet or gold,
And you carry away of the treasure that
      rains
    As much as your apron can hold!
So come, little child, cuddle close to me
    In your dainty white nightcap and gown,
And I'll rock you away to that Sugarplum
      Tree
    In the garden of Shut-eye Town.

Eugene Field

THE KITTEN AND
THE FALLING LEAVES

See the kitten on the wall,
Sporting with the leaves that fall!
Withered leaves, one, two, and three,
From the lofty elder-tree.
Through the calm and frosty air
Of this morning bright and fair,
Eddying round and round they sink
Softly, slowly. One might think,
From the motions that are made,
Every little leaf conveyed
Some small fairy, hither tending,
To this lower world descending.
— But the kitten, how she starts!
Crouches, stretches, paws, and darts!
First at one, and then its fellow,
Just as light, and just as yellow.
There are many now — now one —
Now they stop and there are none.
What intentness of desire
In her upturned eye of fire!
With a tiger leap halfway,
Now she meets the coming prey.
Lets it go at last, and then
Has it in her power again.

William Wordsworth

THE LITTLE ELFMAN

I met a little elfman once,
    Down where the lilies blow.
I asked him why he was so small,
    And why he didn't grow.

He slightly frowned, and with his eye
    He looked me through and through —
"I'm just as big for me," said he,
    "As you are big for you!"

John Kendrick Bangs

THE LILY PRINCESS

Down from her dainty head
The Lily Princess lightly drops
A spider's airy thread.

GOOD MORNING,
MERRY SUNSHINE

Good morning, merry sunshine,
How did you wake so soon?
You've scared the little stars away,
And shined away the moon;
I saw you go to sleep last night,
Before I ceased my playing.
How did you get 'way over here,
And where have you been staying?

I never go to sleep, dear;
I just go round to see
My little children of the East
Who rise and watch for me.
I waken all the birds and bees,
And flowers on the way,
And last of all the little child
Who stayed out late to play.

THE CITY MOUSE AND THE
GARDEN MOUSE

The city mouse lives in a house;
    The garden mouse lives in a bower,
He's friendly with the frogs and toads,
    And sees the pretty plants in flower.

The city mouse eats bread and cheese;
    The garden mouse eats what he can;
We will not grudge him seeds and stocks,
    Poor little timid furry man.

Christina Rossetti

25

TREES

The oak is called the king of trees;
The aspen quivers in the breeze;
The poplar grows up straight and tall;
The pear tree spreads along the wall;
The sycamore gives pleasant shade;
The willow droops in watery glade;
The fir tree useful timber gives;
The beech amid the forest lives.

Sara Coleridge

THE MOUNTAIN AND THE SQUIRREL

The mountain and the squirrel
Had a quarrel,
And the former called the latter "Little prig":
Bun replied,
"You are doubtless very big;
But all sorts of things and weather
Must be taken in together
To make up a year,
And a sphere.
And I think it no disgrace
To occupy my place.
If I'm not so large as you,
You are not so small as I,
And not half so spry.
I'll not deny you make
A very pretty squirrel track.
Talents differ; all is well and wisely put,
If I cannot carry forests on my back,
Neither can you crack a nut."

Ralph Waldo Emerson

HOW THEY SLEEP

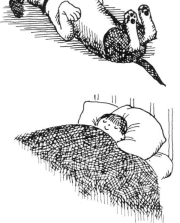

Some things go to sleep in such a funny way:
Little birds stand on one leg and tuck their heads
    away;

Chickens do the same, standing on their perch;
Little mice lie soft and still, as if they were in
    church;

Kittens curl up close in such a funny ball;
Horses hang their sleepy heads and stand still in
    a stall;

Sometimes dogs stretch out, or curl up in a heap;
Cows lie down upon their sides when they would
    go to sleep.

But little babies dear are snugly tucked in beds,
Warm with blankets, all so soft, and pillows for
    their heads.

Bird and beast and babe — I wonder which of all
Dream the dearest dreams that down from
    dreamland fall!

FOUR DUCKS ON A POND

    Four ducks on a pond,
    A grass bank beyond,
    A blue sky of spring,
    White clouds on the wing;
    What a little thing
    To remember for years —
    To remember with tears!

        William Allingham

SUSAN BLUE

    Oh, Susan Blue,
      How do you do?
   Please may I go for a walk with you?
      Where shall we go?
      Oh, I know —
   Down in the meadow where the cowslips
        grow!

        Kate Greenaway

CERTAINTY

I never saw a moor,
I never saw the sea;
Yet know I how the heather looks,
And what a wave must be.

I never spoke with God,
Nor visited in Heaven;
Yet certain am I of the spot
As if the chart were given.

Emily Dickinson

A CRADLE SONG

Golden slumbers kiss your eyes,
Smiles awake you when you rise.
Sleep, pretty wantons, do not cry,
And I will sing a lullaby:
Rock them, rock them, lullaby.

Care is heavy, therefore, sleep you;
You are care, and care must keep you.
Sleep, pretty wantons, do not cry,
And I will sing a lullaby:
Rock them, rock them, lullaby.

Thomas Dekker

OLD DOG

OLD DOG,
Why do you lie so still?
Are you thinking of when you were a pup?
Are you longing to be a pup?

OLD DOG,
Why do you lie so still?
Do you remember your mother?
Do you want your mother near you?

OLD DOG,
Why do you lie so still?
You must be dreaming of childhood.
You must be afraid to die.

OLD DOG,
Why do you lie so still?
Will you never wake up?
Won't you ever wake up?

Ann Covici

29

THE MONTHS

January brings the snow,
Makes our feet and fingers glow.

February brings the rain,
Thaws the frozen lake again.

May brings flocks of pretty lambs,
Skipping by their fleecy dams.

June brings tulips, lilies, roses,
Fills the children's hands with posies.

Warm September brings the fruit;
Sportsmen then begin to shoot.

Fresh October brings the pheasant;
Then to gather nuts is pleasant.

March brings breezes loud and shrill,
Stirs the dancing daffodil.

April brings the primrose sweet,
Scatters daisies at our feet.

Hot July brings cooling showers,
Apricots and gillyflowers.

August brings the sheaves of corn;
Then the harvest home is borne.

Dull November brings the blast,
When the leaves are whirling fast.

Chill December brings the sleet,
Blazing fires and Christmas treat.

Sara Coleridge

THE GRASSHOPPER
AND THE ELEPHANT

Way down south where bananas grow,
A grasshopper stepped on an elephant's
    toe.
The elephant said, with tears in his eyes,
"Pick on somebody your own size."

THE OWL AND THE PUSSYCAT

The Owl and the Pussycat went to sea
    In a beautiful pea-green boat;
They took some honey, and plenty of money
    Wrapped up in a five-pound note.
The Owl looked up to the stars above,
    And sang to a small guitar,
"O lovely Pussy, O Pussy, my love,
    What a beautiful Pussy you are,
      You are,
      You are!
    What a beautiful Pussy you are!"

Pussy said to the Owl, "You elegant fowl,
    How charmingly sweet you sing!
Oh! let us be married; too long we have
      tarried:
    But what shall we do for a ring?"
They sailed away, for a year and a day,
    To the land where the bong-tree grows,
And there in a wood a Piggy-wig stood,
    With a ring at the end of his nose,
      His nose,
      His nose,
    With a ring at the end of his nose.

"Dear Pig, are you willing to sell for one
      shilling
    Your ring?" Said the Piggy, "I will."
So they took it away, and were married next
      day
    By the turkey who lives on the hill.
They dined on mince and slices of quince,
    Which they ate with a runcible spoon;
And hand in hand, on the edge of the sand,
    They danced by the light of the moon,
      The moon,
      The moon,
    They danced by the light of the moon.

Edward Lear

SAILING

I see a ship a-sailing, sailing, sailing,
I see a ship a-sailing, sailing out to sea;
The captain at the railing, railing, railing,
The captain at the railing waves his hand to me.

I see a ship a-rolling, rolling, rolling,
I see a ship a-rolling, rolling home from sea;
I hear its bell a-tolling, tolling, tolling,
I hear its bell a-tolling, coming back to me.

TO SEE A WORLD

To see a world in a grain of sand
And a heaven in a wild flower,
Hold Infinity in the palm of your hand
And Eternity in an hour.

William Blake

THE ROCK

By a flat rock on the shore of the sea
My dear one spoke to me. Wild thyme
Now grows by the rock
And a sprig of rosemary.

36

A SEA SONG FROM THE SHORE

Hail! Ho!
Sail! Ho!
Ahoy! Ahoy! Ahoy!
Who calls to me,
So far at sea?
Only a little boy!

Sail! Ho!
Hail! Ho!
The sailor he sails the sea:
I wish he would capture
A little sea horse
And send him home to me.

I wish, as he sails
Through the tropical gales
He would catch me a sea bird, too,
With its silver wings
And the song it sings,
And its breast of down and dew!

I wish he would catch me
A little mermaid,
Some island where he lands,
With her dripping curls,
And her crown of pearls,
And the looking glass in her hands!

Hail! Ho!
Sail! Ho!
Sail far o'er the fabulous main!
And if I were a sailor,
I'd sail with you,
Though I never sailed back again.

James Whitcomb Riley

37

THE FAIRIES

Up the airy mountain,
      Down the rushy glen,
We daren't go a-hunting,
      For fear of little men.
Wee folk, good folk,
      Trooping all together;
Green jacket, red cap,
      And white owl's feather!

Down along the rocky shore
      Some make their home.
They live on crispy pancakes
      Of yellow tide-foam;
Some in the reeds
      Of the black mountain lake,
With frogs for their watchdogs,
      All night awake.

William Allingham

THE VIOLET

A violet by a mossy stone,
Half hidden from the eye,
Fair as a star, when only one
Is shining in the sky.

William Wordsworth

W

The King sent for his wise men all
    To find a rhyme for W.
When they had thought a good long time
But could not think of a single rhyme,
    "I'm sorry," said he, "to trouble you."

James Reeves

ONE MARCH DAY

As I went walking, one March day,
    Down the length of Blossom Street,
Round me whirled a wind at play,
    And lifted me right off my feet.

English Rhyme

A CENTIPEDE

A centipede was happy quite
Until a frog in fun
Said, "Pray, which leg comes after which?"
This raised her mind to such a pitch,
She lay distracted in a ditch,
Considering how to run.

A KITE

I often sit and wish that I
Could be a kite up in the sky,
And ride upon the breeze and go
Whichever way I chanced to blow.
Then I could look beyond the town,
And see the river winding down,
And follow all the ships that sail
Like me before the merry gale,
Until at last with them I came
To some place with a foreign name.

Frank Dempster Sherman

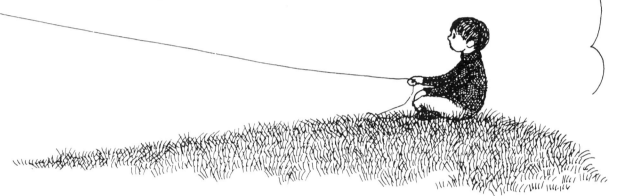

PEDIGREE

The pedigree of honey
Does not concern the bee;
A clover, any time, to him
Is aristocracy.

Emily Dickinson

MY VALENTINE

I will make you brooches and toys for your delight
Of bird song at morning and starshine at night.
I will make a palace fit for you and me,
  Of green days in forests
  And blue days at sea.

Robert Louis Stevenson

CARPENTERS

Saw, saw, saw away,
Saw the boards and saw the timbers.
Saw, saw, saw away,
We will build a house today.

41

THE DUEL

The gingham dog and the calico cat
Side by side on the table sat;
'Twas half-past twelve, and (what do you think!)
Nor one nor t' other had slept a wink!
   The old Dutch clock and the Chinese plate
   Appeared to know as sure as fate
There was going to be a terrible spat.
    (I wasn't there; I simply state
    What was told to me by the Chinese plate!)

The gingham dog went, "Bow-wow-wow!"
And the calico cat replied, "Mee-ow!"
The air was littered, an hour or so,
With bits of gingham and calico,
   While the old Dutch clock in the chimney-place
   Up with its hands before its face,
For it always dreaded a family row!
    (Now mind: I'm only telling you
    What the old Dutch clock declares is true!)

The Chinese plate looked very blue,
And wailed, "Oh, dear! what shall we do!"
But the gingham dog and the calico cat
Wallowed this way and tumbled that,
   Employing every tooth and claw
   In the awfullest way you ever saw —
And, oh! how the gingham and calico flew!
    (Don't fancy I exaggerate —
    I got my news from the Chinese plate!)

Next morning, where the two had sat
They found no trace of dog or cat;
And some folks think unto this day
That burglars stole that pair away!
   But the truth about the cat and pup
   Is this: they ate each other up!
Now what do you really think of that!
    (The old Dutch clock it told me so,
    And that is how I came to know.)

            Eugene Field

THE MILK JUG

(The Kitten Speaks)

The Gentle Milk Jug blue and white
    I love with all my soul;
She pours herself with all her might
    To fill my breakfast bowl.

All day she sits upon the shelf,
    She does not jump or climb —
She only waits to pour herself
    When 'tis my suppertime.

And when the Jug is empty quite,
    I shall not mew in vain,
The Friendly Cow all red and white,
    Will fill her up again.

Oliver Herford

CHOOSING A KITTEN

A black-nosed kitten will slumber all the day;
A white-nosed kitten is ever glad to play;
A yellow-nosed kitten will answer to your call;
And a gray-nosed kitten I like best of all.

I HAD A LITTLE DOGGY

I had a little Doggy that used to sit and beg;
But Doggy tumbled down the stairs and broke his little leg.
Oh! Doggy, I will nurse you, and try to make you well,
And you shall have a collar with a little silver bell.

Ah! Doggy, don't you think that you should very faithful be,
For having such a loving friend to comfort you as me?
And when your leg is better, and you can run and play,
We'll have a scamper in the fields and see them making hay.

But, Doggy, you must promise (and mind your word to keep)
Not once to tease the little lambs, or run among the sheep;
And then the little yellow chicks that play upon the grass,
You must not even wag your tail to scare them as you pass.

WHAT DOES LITTLE BIRDIE SAY?

What does little birdie say,
In her nest at peep of day?
"Let me fly," says little birdie,
    "Mother, let me fly away."
"Birdie, rest a little longer,
Till the little wings are stronger."
So she rests a little longer,
    Then she flies away.

What does little baby say,
In her bed at peep of day?
Baby says, like little birdie,
    "Let me rise and fly away."
"Baby, sleep a little longer,
Till the little limbs are stronger."
If she sleeps a little longer,
    Baby, too, shall fly away.

Alfred, Lord Tennyson

THE OAK

Live thy life,
    Young and old,
Like yon oak,
Bright in spring,
    Living gold;

Summer-rich
    Then; and then
Autumn-changed,
Soberer-hued
    Gold again.

All his leaves
    Fallen at length,
Look, he stands,
Trunk and bough,
    Naked strength.

Alfred, Lord Tennyson

HEIGH HO!

Heigh Ho! Time creeps but slow;
    I've looked up the hill so long;
None come this way, the sun sinks low,
    And my shadow's very long.

Kate Greenaway

44

THE BROOMSTICK TRAIN

Look out! Look out, boys! Clear the track!
The witches are here! They've all come back!
They hanged them high. No use! No use!
What cares a witch for the hangman's noose?
They buried them deep, but they wouldn't lie still,
For cats and witches are hard to kill;
They swore they shouldn't and wouldn't die —
Books said they did, but they lie! they lie!

Oliver Wendell Holmes

THE CLUCKING HEN

"Will you take a walk with me,
    My little wife, today?
There's barley in the barley field,
    And hayseed in the hay."

"Thank you," said the clucking hen.
    "I've something else to do;
I'm busy sitting on my eggs,
    I cannot walk with you."

The clucking hen sat on her nest,
    She made it on the hay;
And warm and snug beneath her breast
    A dozen white eggs lay.

CRACK! CRACK! went all the eggs,
    Out dropped the chickens small.
"Cluck!" said the clucking hen.
    "Now I have you all.

Come along, my little chicks,
    I'll take a walk with you."
"Hello!" said the rooster.
    "Cock-a-doodle-doo!"

ALWAYS FINISH

If a task is once begun,
Never leave it till it's done.
Be the labor great or small,
Do it well or not at all.

THE MOON SHIP

In the ocean of the sky,
Borne on rising waves of cloud,
The moon ship
Goes a-gliding by
Through a forest of stars.

From the Japanese.

NIGHT BLESSING

Good night,
Sleep tight,
Wake up bright
In the morning light
To do what's right
With all your might.

SWEET AND LOW

Sweet and low, sweet and low,
    Wind of the western sea!
Low, low, breathe and blow,
    Wind of the western sea!
Over the rolling waters go,
Come from the dying moon, and blow,
    Blow him again to me;
While my little one, while my pretty one
    sleeps.

Sleep and rest, sleep and rest,
    Father will come to thee soon;
Rest, rest, on Mother's breast,
    Father will come to thee soon;
Father will come to his babe in the nest,
Silver sails all out of the west
    Under the silver moon:
Sleep, my little one, sleep, my pretty one,
    sleep.

Alfred, Lord Tennyson

THE ICHTHYOSAURUS

There once was an Ichthyosaurus
Who lived when the earth was all porous,
But he fainted with shame
When he first heard his name,
And departed a long time before us.

CATERPILLAR

Brown and furry
Caterpillar in a hurry
Take your walk
To the shady leaf, or stalk,
Or what not,
Which may be the chosen spot.
No toad spy you,
Hovering bird of prey pass by you;
Spin and die,
To live again a butterfly.

Christina Rossetti

A RULE FOR BIRDS' NESTERS

The robin and the redbreast,
　The robin and the wren;
If ye take out o' their nest,
　Ye'll never thrive agen!

The robin and the redbreast,
　The martin and the swallow;
If ye touch one o' their eggs,
　Bad luck will surely follow!

THE YOUNG LADY OF NIGER

There was a young lady of Niger
Who smiled as she rode on a tiger;
　They returned from the ride
　With the lady inside,
And the smile on the face of the tiger.

A BIRD

A bird came down the walk:
He did not know I saw;
He bit an angleworm in halves
And ate the fellow, raw.

And then he drank a dew
From a convenient grass,
And then hopped sidewise to the wall
To let a beetle pass.

Emily Dickinson

49

WHO HAS SEEN THE WIND?

Who has seen the wind?
    Neither I nor you;
But when the leaves hang trembling,
    The wind is passing through.

Who has seen the wind?
    Neither you nor I:
But when the trees bow down their heads,
    The wind is passing by.

Christina Rossetti

THE FRIENDLY COW

The friendly cow, all red and white,
    I love with all my heart;
She gives me cream, with all her might,
    To eat with apple tart.

She wanders lowing here and there,
    And yet she cannot stray,
All in the pleasant open air,
    The pleasant light of day.

And blown by all the winds that pass
    And wet with all the showers,
She walks among the meadow grass
    And eats the meadow flowers.

Robert Louis Stevenson

LITTLE WIND

Little wind, blow on the hilltop;
Little wind, blow on the plain,
Little wind, blow up the sunshine,
Little wind, blow off the rain.

THE TWENTY-FOURTH OF DECEMBER

The clock ticks slowly, slowly in the hall,
And slower and more slow the long hours crawl;
It seems as though today
Would never pass away;
The clock ticks slowly, s-l-o-w-l-y in the hall.

SNOWFLAKES

Out of the bosom of the air,
    Out of the cloud-folds of her garments shaken,
Over the woodland brown and bare,
    Over the harvest fields forsaken,
Silent, and soft, and slow
    Descends the snow.

Henry Wadsworth Longfellow

MY GIFT

What can I give Him,
Poor as I am;
If I were a shepherd,
I would give Him a lamb.
If I were a wise man,
I would do my part.
But what can I give Him?
I will give my heart.

Christina Rossetti

52

AN OLD CHRISTMAS GREETING

Sing hey! Sing hey!
For Christmas Day,
Twine mistletoe and holly,
For friendship glows
In winter snows,
And so let's all be jolly.

Nursery Rhyme

CHRISTMAS HEARTH RHYME

Sing we all merrily,
    Christmas is here,
The day we love best
    Of all days in the year.

Bring forth the holly,
    The box and the bay,
Deck out our cottage
    For glad Christmas day.

Sing we all merrily,
    Draw near the fire,
Sister and brother,
    Grandson and sire.

Old English

CHRISTMAS IN THE OLDEN TIME

Heap on more wood! The wind is chill;
But let it whistle as it will.
We'll keep our Christmas merry still.

Sir Walter Scott

53

WINTER

Bread and milk for breakfast,
    And woolen frocks to wear,
And a crumb for robin redbreast
    On the cold days of the year.

Christina Rossetti

CHRISTMAS BELLS

I heard the bells on Christmas Day
Their old, familiar carols play,
    And wild and sweet
    The words repeat
Of peace on earth, good will to men!

And thought how, as the day had come,
The belfries of all Christendom
    Had rolled along
    The unbroken song
Of peace on earth, good will to men!

Till, ringing, singing, on its way,
The world revolved from night to day,
    A voice, a chime,
    A chant sublime
Of peace on earth, good will to men!

Henry Wadsworth Longfellow

SANTA CLAUS AND THE MOUSE

One Christmas, when Santa Claus
   Came to a certain house,
To fill the children's stockings there,
   He found a little mouse.

"A Merry Christmas, little friend,"
   Said Santa good and kind.
"The same to you, sir," said the mouse,
   "I thought you wouldn't mind,

If I should stay awake tonight
   And watch you for a while."
"You're very welcome, little mouse,"
   Said Santa, with a smile.

And then he filled the stockings up
   Before the mouse could wink —
From toe to top, from top to toe,
   There wasn't left a chink.

"Now they won't hold another thing,"
   Said Santa Claus with pride.
A twinkle came in mouse's eyes,
   But humbly he replied :

"It's not polite to contradict —
   Your pardon I implore —
But in the fullest stocking there
   I could put one thing more."

"Oh, ho!" laughed Santa. "Silly mouse,
　　Don't I know how to pack?
By filling stockings all these years
　　I should have learned the knack."

And then he took the stocking down
　　From where it hung so high,
And said, "Now put in one thing more,
　　I give you leave to try."

The mousie chuckled to himself,
　　And then he softly stole
Right to the stocking's crowded toe
　　And gnawed a little hole!

"Now, if you please, good Santa Claus,
　　I've put in one thing more,
For you will own that little hole
　　Was not in there before."

How Santa Claus did laugh and laugh!
　　And then he gaily spoke,
"Well, you shall have a Christmas cheese
　　For that nice little joke!"

If you don't think this story is true,
　　Why, I can show to you
The very stocking with the hole
　　The little mouse gnawed through!

Emilie Poulsson

DAFFODILS

I wandered lonely as a cloud
That floats on high o'er vales and hills,
When all at once I saw a crowd —
A host of golden daffodils
Beside the lake, beneath the trees,
Fluttering and dancing in the breeze.

Continuous as the stars that shine
And twinkle on the Milky Way,
They stretched in never-ending line
Along the margin of a bay:
Ten thousand saw I, at a glance,
Tossing their heads in sprightly dance.

The waves beside them danced, but they
Out-did the sparkling waves in glee:
A poet could not but be gay,
In such a jocund company:
I gazed — and gazed — but little thought
What wealth the show to me had brought:

For oft, when on my couch I lie
In vacant or in pensive mood,
They flash upon that inward eye
Which is the bliss of solitude;
And then my heart with pleasure fills,
And dances with the daffodils.

William Wordsworth

THE ELF AND THE DORMOUSE

Under a toadstool crept a wee elf,
Out of the rain, to shelter himself.

Under the toadstool, sound asleep,
Sat a big dormouse all in a heap.

Trembled the wee elf, frightened, and yet
Fearing to fly away lest he get wet.

To the next shelter — maybe a mile!
Sudden the wee elf smiled a wee smile,

Tugged till the toadstool toppled in two,
Holding it over him, gayly he flew.

Soon he was safe home, dry as could be,
Soon woke the dormouse — "Good gracious me!

Where is my toadstool?" loud he lamented.
And that's how umbrellas first were invented.

Oliver Herford

RAIN

The rain is raining all around,
    It falls on field and tree;
It rains on the umbrellas here,
    And on the ships at sea.

Robert Louis Stevenson

APRIL FOOL'S DAY

The first of April, some do say,
Is set apart for All Fools' day,
But why the people call it so
Nor I, nor they themselves, do know.

Old English Almanac

SWEET PEAS

Here are sweet peas, on tiptoe for a flight,
With wings of gentle flush o'er delicate white,
And taper fingers catching at all things,
To bind them all about with tiny rings.

John Keats

"CROAK!" SAID THE TOAD

"Croak!" said the toad. "I'm hungry, I think.
Today I've had nothing to eat or to drink.
I'll crawl to a garden and jump through the pales,
And there I'll dine nicely on slugs and on snails."

"Ho, ho!" quoth the frog. "Is that what you mean?
Then I'll hop away to the next meadow stream.
There I will drink, and eat worms and slugs, too,
And then I shall have a good dinner like you."

Old Garden Rhyme

THE SWAN

Swan swam over the sea —
    Swim, swan, swim;
Swan swam back again,
    Well swam, swan.

GO TO THE ANT

Go to the ant, thou sluggard;
Consider her ways, and be wise:
Which having no guide,
Overseer, or ruler,
Provideth her meat in the summer,
And gathereth her food in the harvest.

The Book of Proverbs

OLD DAME CRICKET

Old Dame Cricket, down in the thicket,
Brought up her children nine —
    Queer little chaps, in glossy black caps
And brown little suits so fine.

    "My children," she said,
    "The birds are abed:
Go and make the dark earth glad!
    Chirp while you can!"
    And then she began,
Till, oh, what a concert they had!

    They hopped with delight,
    They chirped all night,
Singing, "Cheer up! Cheer up! Cheer!"
    Old Dame Cricket,
    Down in the thicket,
Sat awake till dawn to hear.

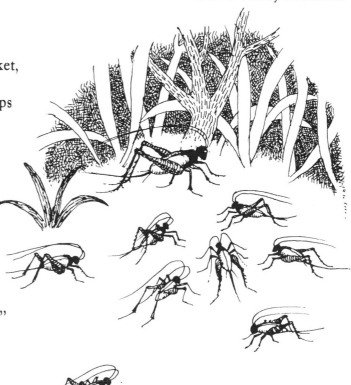

A BOY'S SONG

Where the pools are bright and deep,
Where the gray trout lies asleep,
Up the river, and over the lea,
That's the way for Billy and me.

Where the blackbird sings the latest,
Where the hawthorne blooms the sweetest,
Where the nestlings chirp and flee,
That's the way for Billy and me.

Where the mowers mow the cleanest,
Where the hay lies thick and greenest;
There to trace the homeward bee,
That's the way for Billy and me.

Where the hazel bank is steepest,
Where the shadow falls the deepest,
Where the clustering nuts fall free,
That's the way for Billy and me.

James Hogg

Eenie, meenie, minie, mo,
Catch a tiger by the toe,
If he hollers, let him go,
Eenie, meenie, minie, mo.

Out goes the rat,
Out goes the cat,
Out goes the lady
With the big green hat.
Y, O, U, spells you;
O, U, T, spells out!

One potato, two potato,
Three potato, four;
Five potato, six potato,
Seven potato, MORE.

One-ery, Two-ery, Ickery, Ann,
Phillip-son, Phollop-son, Nicholas, John,
    Queevy, Quavy,
    English Navy,
Zinglum, Zanglum, Bolun, Bun.

Hinty, minty, cuty, corn,
Apple seed and apple thorn,
Wire, briar, limber lock,
Three geese in a flock.
One flew east, and one flew west,
One flew over the cuckoo's nest.

THE BEE

There is a little gentleman
 That wears yellow clothes;
And a dirk below his doublet,
 For sticking of his foes.

He's in a stinging posture
 Wherever him you see,
And if you offer violence,
 He'll stab his dirk in thee.

THE BAREFOOT BOY

Blessings on thee, little man,
Barefoot boy, with cheeks of tan!
With thy turned-up pantaloons,
And thy merry whistled tunes;
With thy red lip, redder still
Kissed by strawberries on the hill;
With the sunshine on thy face,
Through thy torn brim's jaunty grace;
From my heart I give thee joy —
I was once a barefoot boy!

John Greenleaf Whittier

THE MELANCHOLY PIG

There was a pig that sat alone,
 Beside a ruined pump.
By day and night he made his moan:
 It would have stirred a heart of stone
To see him wring his hoofs and groan,
 Because he could not jump.

Lewis Carroll

A YOUNG LADY NAMED BRIGHT

There was a young lady named Bright,
Who traveled much faster than light.
 She started one day
 In the relative way,
And returned on the previous night.

ANNIE'S GARDEN

In little Annie's garden
  Grew all sorts of posies;
There were pinks, and mignonette,
  And tulips, and roses.

Sweet peas, and morning glories,
  A bed of violets blue,
And marigolds, and asters,
  In Annie's garden grew.

There the bees went for honey,
  And the hummingbirds, too;
And there the pretty butterflies
  And the ladybirds flew.

And there among her flowers,
  Every bright and pleasant day,
In her own pretty garden
  Little Annie went to play.

Eliza Lee Follen

IRIS

Ere yet the sun is high,
All blue the iris blossoms wave,
  The color of the sky.

From the Japanese.

THE SNAIL'S DREAM

A snail who had a way, it seems,
Of dreaming very curious dreams,
Once dream't he was — you'll never guess! —
The Lightning Limited Express.

Oliver Herford

WHAT ROBIN TOLD

How do robins build their nests?
   Robin Redbreast told me —
First a wisp of yellow hay
In a pretty round they lay;

Then some shreds of downy floss,
Feathers, too, and bits of moss,
Woven with a sweet, sweet song,
This way, that way, and across;
   THAT'S what Robin told me.

Where do robins hide their nests?
   Robin Redbreast told me —
Up among the leaves so deep,
Where the sunbeams rarely creep,
Long before the leaves are gold,
Bright-eyed stars will peep and see
Baby robins — one, two, three;
   THAT'S what Robin told me.

George Cooper

THREE LITTLE TREES

A dear little secret,
As sweet as could be,
The breeze told one day
To the glad apple tree.
The breeze told the apple,
The apple the plum,
The plum told the pear,
"Robin Redbreast has come."

HOW MARIGOLDS CAME YELLOW

Jealous girls these sometimes were,
While they lived, or lasted here:
Turned to flowers, still they be
Yellow, marked for jealousy.

Robert Herrick

THE DAY IS DONE

The day is done, and the darkness
  Falls from the wings of Night,
As a feather is wafted downward
  From an eagle in his flight.

I see the lights of the village
  Gleam through the rain and the mist,
And a feeling of sadness comes o'er me
  That my soul cannot resist:

A feeling of sadness and longing,
  That is not akin to pain,
And resembles sorrow only
  As the mist resembles the rain.

Come, read to me some poem,
  Some simple and heartfelt lay,
That shall soothe this restless feeling,
  And banish the thoughts of day.

Not from the grand old masters,
  Not from the bards sublime,
Whose distant footsteps echo
  Through the corridors of Time.

For, like strains of martial music,
  Their mighty thoughts suggest
Life's endless toil and endeavor;
  And tonight I long for rest.

Read from some humbler poet,
  Whose songs gushed from his heart,
As showers from the clouds of summer,
  Or tears from the eyelids start;

Who, through long days of labor,
  And nights devoid of ease,
Still heard in his soul the music
  Of wonderful melodies.

Such songs have power to quiet
  The restless pulse of care,
And come like a benediction
  That follows after prayer.

Then read from the treasured volume
  The poem of thy choice,
And lend to the rhyme of the poet
  The beauty of thy voice.

And the night shall be filled with music,
  And the cares that infest the day,
Shall fold their tents, like the Arabs,
  And as silently steal away.

          Henry Wadsworth Longfellow

THE KAYAK

Over the briny wave I go,
In spite of the weather, in spite of the snow:
What cares the hardy Eskimo?
In my little skiff, with paddle and lance,
I glide where the foaming billows dance.

Round me the sea-birds slip and soar;
Like me, they love the ocean's roar.
Sometimes a floating iceberg gleams
Above me with its melting streams;
Sometimes a rushing wave will fall
Down on my skiff and cover it all.

But what care I for a wave's attack?
With my paddle I right my little kayak,
And then its weight I speedily trim,
And over the water away I skim.

TONY O

Over the bleak and barren snow
A voice there came a-calling;
"Where are you going to, Tony O!
Where are you going this morning?"

"I am going where there are rivers of wine,
The mountains bread and honey:
There Kings and Queens do mind the swine,
And the poor have all the money."

Colin Francis

DOLL'S WALK

I took my dolly for a walk.
Before we reached the gate,
She kicked her little slipper off,
And soon she lost the mate.

THE WEST WIND

The trumpet of a prophecy! O Wind,
If winter comes, can spring be far behind?

Percy Bysshe Shelley

THE SNOWMAN

Once there was a snowman
 Stood outside the door
Thought he'd like to come inside
 And run around the floor;
Thought he'd like to warm himself
 By the firelight red;
Thought he'd like to climb up
 On that big white bed.
So he called the North Wind, "Help me now, I pray.
 I'm completely frozen, standing here all day."
So the North Wind came along and blew him in the door,
 And now there's nothing left of him
But a puddle on the floor!

INSCRIBED ON THE COLLAR OF A DOG

I am his Highness' dog at Kew;
Pray tell me, sir — whose dog are you?

Alexander Pope

OLD SONG

Haste thee, Winter, haste away!
Far too long has been thy stay.

English Couplet

ONE STORMY NIGHT

Two little kittens,
  One stormy night,
Began to quarrel,
  And then to fight.

One had a mouse,
  The other had none;
And that's the way
  The quarrel begun.

"I'LL have that mouse,"
  Said the bigger cat.
"YOU'LL have that mouse?
  We'll see about that!"

"I WILL have that mouse,"
  Said the eldest son.
"You SHA'NT have the mouse,"
  Said the little one.

The old woman seized
  Her sweeping broom,
And swept both kittens
  Right out of the room.

The ground was covered
  With frost and snow,
And the two little kittens
  Had nowhere to go.

They lay and shivered
  On a mat at the door
While the old woman
  Was sweeping the floor.

And then they crept in,
  As quiet as mice,
All wet with the snow,
  And as cold as ice,

And found it much better,
  That stormy night,
To lie by the fire
  Than to quarrel and fight.

Traditional

QUEEN MAB

A little fairy comes at night,
Her eyes are blue, her hair is brown,
With silver spots upon her wings,
And from the moon she flutters down.

She has a little silver wand,
And when a good child goes to bed
She waves her hand from right to left,
And makes a circle round its head.

And then it dreams of pleasant things,
Of fountains filled with fairy fish,
And trees that bear delicious fruit,
And bow their branches at a wish:

Of arbors filled with dainty scents
From lovely flowers that never fade;
Bright flies that glitter in the sun,
And glowworms shining in the shade:

And talking birds with gifted tongues,
For singing songs and telling tales,
And pretty dwarfs to show the way
Through fairy hills and fairy dales.

Thomas Hood

THE MAY QUEEN

You must wake and call me early, call me early, Mother dear;
Tomorrow'll be the happiest time of all the glad new year;
Of all the glad new year, Mother, the maddest, merriest day,
For I'm to be Queen o' the May, Mother, I'm to be Queen o' the May.

Alfred, Lord Tennyson

HERE WE COME A-PIPING

Here we come a-piping,
In springtime and in May;
Green fruit a-ripening,
And winter fled away.
The Queen she sits upon the strand,
Fair as lily, white as wand;
Seven billows on the sea,
Horses riding fast and free,
And bells beyond the sand.

WILD BEASTS

I will be a lion
    And you shall be a bear,
And each of us will have a den
    Beneath a nursery chair;
And you must growl and growl and growl,
    And I will roar and roar,
And then — why, then — you'll growl again,
    And I will roar some more!

Evaleen Stein

THE NAUGHTY BOY

There was a naughty boy,
    And a naughty boy was he,
He ran away to Scotland
    The people for to see —
        Then he found
        That the ground
        Was as hard,
        That a yard
        Was as long,
        That a song
        Was as merry,
        That a cherry
        Was as red,
        That lead
        Was as weighty,
        That fourscore
        Was as eighty,
        That a door
        Was as wooden
        As in England —
So he stood in his shoes
        And he wondered,
        He wondered.
He stood in his shoes
        And he wondered.

John Keats

TO AN INSECT

Thou art a female, katydid!
    I know it by the trill
That quivers through thy piercing notes,
    So petulant and shrill;
I think there is a knot of you
    Beneath the hollow tree —
A knot of spinster katydids —
    Do katydids drink tea?

Oliver Wendell Holmes

FERRY ME ACROSS
THE WATER

"Ferry me across the water,
    Do, boatman, do."
"If you've a penny in your purse,
    I'll ferry you."

"I have a penny in my purse,
    And my eyes are blue;
So ferry me across the water,
    Do, boatman, do!"

"Step into my ferryboat,
    Be they black or blue,
And for the penny in your purse
    I'll ferry you."

Christina Rossetti

WHAT IS PINK? A ROSE IS PINK

What is pink? A rose is pink
    By the fountain's brink.
What is red? A poppy's red
    In its barley bed.
What is blue? The sky is blue
    Where the clouds float thro'.
What is white? A swan is white
    Sailing in the light.
What is yellow? A pear is yellow,
    Rich and ripe and mellow.
What is green? The grass is green
    With small flowers between.
What is violet? Clouds are violet
    In the summer twilight,
What is orange? Why, an orange,
    Just an orange!

Christina Rossetti

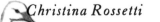

MY FAIRY

I'd like to tame a fairy,
  To keep it on a shelf,
To see it wash its little face,
  And dress its little self.
I'd teach it pretty manners,
  It always should say "Please,"
And then, you know, I'd make it sew,
  And curtsy with its knees!

EXTREMES

A little boy once played so loud
That the thunder, up in a thundercloud,
Said, "Since *I* can't be heard, why, then,
I'll never, never thunder again!"

And a little girl once kept so still
That she heard a fly on the window sill
Whisper and say to a ladybird,
"She's the stillest child I ever heard!"

James Whitcomb Riley

DON'T GIVE UP

If you've tried and have not won,
  Never stop for crying;
All that's great and good is done
  Just by patient trying.

If by easy work you beat,
  Who the more will prize you?
Gaining victory from defeat,
  That's the test that tries you.

Phoebe Cary

THE PANCAKE

Mix a pancake,
Stir a pancake,
  Pop it in the pan;
Fry the pancake,
Toss the pancake —
  Catch it if you can!

Christina Rossetti

80

Tomorrow is Saint Valentine's day,
   All in the morning betime,
And I a maid at your window,
   To be your Valentine.

William Shakespeare

THE LITTLE PEACH

A little peach in the orchard grew —
A little peach of emerald hue;
Warmed by the sun and wet by the dew,
   It grew.

One day, passing the orchard through,
That little peach dawned on the view
Of Johnnie Jones and his sister Sue —
   Those two.

Up at the peach a club he threw —
Down from the tree on which it grew
Fell the little peach of emerald hue —
   Mon dieu!

She took a bite and he a chew,
And then the trouble began to brew —
Trouble the doctor couldn't subdue —
   Too true!

Under the turf where the daisies grew
They planted John and his sister Sue,
And their little souls to the angels flew —
   Boo-hoo!

But what of the peach of emerald hue,
Warmed by the sun and wet by the dew?
Ah, well, its mission on earth was through —
   Adieu!

Eugene Field

THE CROCODILE

How doth the little crocodile
    Improve his shining tail,
And pour the waters of the Nile
    On every golden scale!

How cheerfully he seems to grin,
    How neatly spreads his claws,
And welcomes little fishes in,
    With gently smiling jaws!

Lewis Carroll

WHO IS TAPPING AT MY WINDOW?

"It's not I," said the cat.
"It's not I," said the rat.

"It's not I," said the wren.
"It's not I," said the hen.

"It's not I," said the fox.
"It's not I," said the ox.

"It's not I," said the loon.
"It's not I," said the coon.

"It's not I," said the cony.
"It's not I," said the pony.

"It's not I," said the dog.
"It's not I," said the frog.

"It's not I," said the hare.
"It's not I," said the bear.

"It is I," said the rain,
"Tapping at your windowpane."

A. G. Deming

RAINDROPS

Softly the rain goes pitter-patter,
Softly the rain comes falling down.
Hark to the people who hurry by;
Raindrops are footsteps from out the sky!
Softly the rain goes pitter-patter,
Softly the rain comes falling down.

THE RAIN

The rain came down in torrents
    And Mary said, "Oh, dear,
I'll have to wear my waterproof,
    And rubbers, too, I fear!"
So, carefully protected, she started off for school,
    When the big round sun
Came out and chuckled "April Fool!"

FIVE LITTLE CHICKENS

Said the first little chicken,
With a queer little squirm,
"Oh, I wish I could find
A fat little worm!"

Said the second little chicken,
With an odd little shrug,
"Oh, I wish I could find
A fat little bug!"

Said the third little chicken,
With a little sigh of grief,
"Oh, I wish I could find
A little green leaf!"

Said the fourth little chicken,
With a sharp little squeal,
"Oh, I wish I could find
Some nice yellow meal!"

Said the fifth little chicken,
With a faint little moan,
"I wish I could find
A wee gravel stone!"

"Now, see here," said their mother
From the green garden patch,
"If you want any breakfast,
You must all come and scratch!"

AROUND THE WORLD

In go-cart so tiny
    My sister I drew;
And I've promised to draw her
    The wide world through.

We have not yet started --
    I own it with sorrow --
Because our trip's always
    Put off till tomorrow.

Kate Greenaway

THE VILLAGE BLACKSMITH

Under a spreading chestnut tree
    The village smithy stands;
The smith, a mighty man is he,
    With large and sinewy hands;
And the muscles of his brawny arms
    Are strong as iron bands.

His hair is crisp and black and long,
    His face is like the tan;
His brow is wet with honest sweat,
    He earns whate'er he can,
And looks the whole world in the face,
    For he owes not any man.

Henry Wadsworth Longfellow

DAISIES

At evening when I go to bed,
I see the stars shine overhead;
They are the little daisies white
That dot the meadow of the night.

And often while I'm dreaming so,
Across the sky the moon will go;
It is a lady, sweet and fair,
Who comes to gather daisies there.

For, when at morning I arise,
There's not a star left in the skies;
She's picked them all and dropped them down
Into the meadows of the town.

Frank Dempster Sherman

THE HAPPY SHEEP

All through the night the happy sheep
Lie in the meadow grass asleep.

Their wool keeps out the frost and rain
Until the sun comes round again.

They have no buttons to undo,
Nor hair to brush, like me and you.

And with the light they lift their heads
To find their breakfast on their beds,

Or rise and walk about and eat
The carpet underneath their feet.

Wilfred Thorley

THE BREEZE

Summer breeze so softly blowing,
In my garden pinks are growing;
If you'll go and send the showers,
You may come and smell my flowers.

Old Garden Rhyme

SWAN SONG

Swans sing before they die — 'twere no bad thing
Should certain persons die before they sing.

Samuel Taylor Coleridge

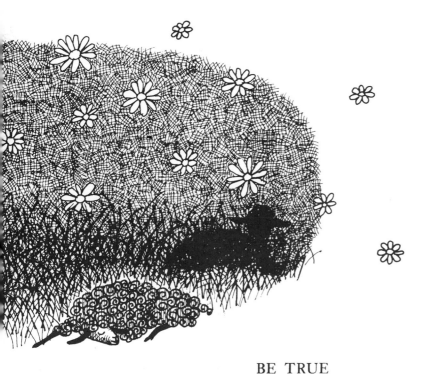

THREE THINGS TO REMEMBER

A Robin Redbreast in a cage
Puts all Heaven in a rage.

A skylark wounded on the wing
Doth make a cherub cease to sing.

He who shall hurt the little wren
Shall never be beloved by men.

William Blake

BE TRUE

To thine own self be true;
And it must follow, as the night the day
Thou cans't not then be false to any man.

William Shakespeare

LITTLE THINGS

Little drops of water,
    Little grains of sand,
Make the mighty ocean
    And the pleasant land.

Thus the little moments,
    Humble though they be,
Make the mighty ages
    Of eternity.

Thus our little errors
    Lead the soul away
From the path of virtue,
    Off in sin to stray.

Little deeds of kindness,
    Little words of love,
Make our earth an Eden,
    Like the heaven above.

Julia A. F. Carney

IN THE MEADOW

In the meadow — what is in the meadow?
Bluebells, buttercups, meadowsweet,
And fairy rings for children's feet,
    In the meadow.

Christina Rossetti

89

THE EAGLE

He clasps the crag with crooked hands;
Close to the sun in lonely lands,
Ringed with the azure world, he stands.

The wrinkled sea beneath him crawls;
He watches from his mountain walls,
And like a thunderbolt he falls.

Alfred, Lord Tennyson

THE SEA GULL

All day long o'er the ocean I fly,
My white wings beating fast through the
    sky,
I hunt fishes all down the bay
And ride on rocking billows in play.

All night long in my rock home I rest,
Away up on a cliff is my nest,
The waves murmur, murmur below,
And winds fresh from the sea o'er me
    blow.

Gaelic Folk Song

TURKEY TIME

Thanksgiving Day will soon be here;
It comes around but once a year.
If I could only have my way,
We'd have Thanksgiving every day!

SING A SONG OF SEASONS

Sing a song of seasons!
    Something bright in all!
Flowers in the summer,
    Fires in the fall!

Robert Louis Stevenson

NOVEMBER

I love the fitful gust that shakes
    The casement all the day,
And from the glossy elm tree takes
    The faded leaves away,
Twirling them by the windowpane
With thousands others down the lane.

I love to see the cottage smoke
    Curl upward through the trees,
The pigeons nestled round the cote,
    November days like these;
The cock upon the woodland crowing,
The mill sails on the heath a-going.

John Clare

AUTUMN

The morns are meeker than they were,
    The nuts are getting brown;
The berry's cheek is plumper,
    The rose is out of town.

The maple wears a gayer scarf,
    The field a scarlet gown.
Lest I should be old-fashioned,
    I'll put a trinket on.

Emily Dickinson

MERRY AUTUMN DAYS

'Tis pleasant on a fine spring morn
    To see the buds expand,
'Tis pleasant in the summertime
    To see the fruitful land;
'Tis pleasant on a winter's night
    To sit around the blaze,
But what are joys like these, my boys,
    To merry autumn days!

We hail the merry autumn days,
    When leaves are turning red;
Because they're far more beautiful
    Than anyone has said.
We hail the merry harvest time,
    The gayest of the year;
The time of rich and bounteous crops,
    Rejoicing and good cheer.

               Charles Dickens

THE FROST SPIRIT

He comes, he comes, the Frost Spirit comes! You may trace his footsteps now
On the naked woods and the blasted fields and the brown hill's withered brow.
He has smitten the leaves of the gray old trees where their pleasant green came forth,
And the winds, which follow wherever he goes, have shaken them down to earth.

               John Greenleaf Whittier

THANKSGIVING DAY

Over the river and through the wood,
    To Grandfather's house we go;
        The horse knows the way
        To carry the sleigh
    Through the white and drifted snow.

Over the river and through the wood —
    Oh, how the wind does blow!
        It stings the toes
        And bites the nose
    As over the ground we go.

Over the river and through the wood,
    To have a first-rate play.
        Hear the bells ring,
        "Ting-a-ling-ding!"
    Hurrah for Thanksgiving Day!

Over the river and through the wood,
    Trot fast, my dapple-gray!
        Spring over the ground
        Like a hunting hound,
    For this is Thanksgiving Day

Over the river and through the wood,
    And straight through the barnyard gate.
        We seem to go
        Extremely slow —
    It is so hard to wait!

Over the river and through the wood —
    Now Grandmother's cap I spy!
        Hurrah for the fun!
        Is the pudding done?
    Hurrah for the pumpkin pie!

Lydia Maria Child

AN OLD RAT'S TALE

He was a rat, and she was a rat,
    And down in one hole they did dwell;
And both were as black as a witch's cat,
    And they loved each other well.

He had a tail and she had a tail,
    Both long and curling and fine;
And each said, "Yours is the finest tail
    In the world, excepting mine."

He smelled the cheese, and she smelled the cheese,
    And they both pronounced it good;
And both remarked it would greatly add
    To the charms of their daily food.

So he ventured out, and she ventured out,
    And I saw them go with pain;
But what befell them I never can tell,
    For they never came back again.

                    Nursery Rhyme

HEARTS AND LACE PAPER

Roses are red, violets blue;
If you will have me, I will have you.
Lilies are white, rosemary's green;
When you are king, I will be queen.

    Gammer Gurton's Garland

HOW ROSES CAME RED

'Tis said, as Cupid danced among
The Gods, he down the nectar flung;
Which, on the white rose being shed,
Made it ever after red.

                    Robert Herrick

SEWING

If Mother Nature patches
    The leaves of trees and vines,
I'm sure she does her darning
    With the needles of the pines;
They are so long and slender,
    And somewhere in full view,
She has her threads of cobweb
    And a thimbleful of dew.

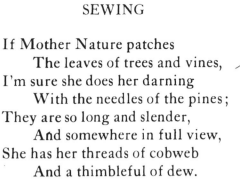

STITCHING

A pocket handkerchief to hem —
    Oh dear, oh dear, oh dear!
How many stitches it will take
    Before it's done, I fear.

Yet set a stitch and then a stitch,
    And stitch and stitch away,
Till stitch by stitch the hem is done —
    And after work is play!

Christina Rossetti

NOT I

Some like drink
    In a pint pot,
Some like to think,
    Some not.

Strong Dutch cheese,
    Old Kentucky Rye,
Some like these;
    Not I.

Some like Poe,
    And others like Scott;
Some like Mrs. Stowe,
    Some not.

Some like to laugh,
    Some like to cry,
Some like to chaff;
    Not I.

Robert Louis Stevenson

EVERY DAY

Love the beautiful,
    Seek out the true,
Wish for the good,
    And the best do!

Felix Mendelssohn

COURAGE

Dare to be true;
    Nothing can need a lie;
The fault that needs one most
    Grows two thereby.

George Herbert

LO, THE WINTER IS PAST

For, lo, the winter is past,
The rain is over and gone;
The flowers appear on the earth;
The time of the singing of birds is come,
And the voice of the turtle is heard in our land.

The Song of Solomon

PIPPA'S SONG

The year's at the spring
And the day's at the morn;
Morning's at seven;
The hillside's dew-pearled;
The lark's on the wing;
The snail's on the thorn:
God's in his heaven —
All's right with the world!

Robert Browning

SPRING

Sound the flute!
Now it's mute.
Birds delight
Day and night;
Nightingale
In the dale,
Lark in sky,
Merrily,
Merrily, merrily, to welcome in the year.

Little boy,
Full of joy;
Little girl,
Sweet and small;
Cock does crow,
So do you;
Merry voice,
Infant noise,
Merrily, merrily, to welcome in the year.

Little lamb
Here I am;
Come and lick
My white neck;
Let me pull
Your soft wool;
Let me kiss
Your soft face;
Merrily, merrily, we welcome in the year.

William Blake

HERE'S TO THEE

Here's to thee,
Old apple tree!
Stand fast root,
Bear well top,
Pray God send us
A youling crop!

Every twig
Apple big;
Every bough
Apple enow;
Hats full, caps full,
Fill quarter sacks full!
Holla, boys, holla!
Huzza!

THE CATS HAVE COME TO TEA

What did she see — oh, what did she see,
As she stood leaning against the tree?
Why, all the cats had come to tea.

What a fine turnout from roundabout!
All the houses had let them out.
And here they were with scamper and shout.

"Mew, mew, mew!" was all they could say,
And, "We hope we find you well today."

Oh, what would she do — oh, what should she do?
What a lot of milk they would get through;
For here they were with, "Mew, mew, mew!"

She did not know — oh, she did not know,
If bread and butter they'd like or no;
They might want little mice, oh! oh! oh!

Dear me — oh, dear me!
All the cats had come to tea.

Kate Greenaway

RAIN IN SUMMER

How beautiful is the rain!
After the dust and heat,
In the broad and fiery street,
In the narrow lane,
How beautiful is the rain!
How it clatters along the roofs,
Like the tramp of hoofs!

How it gushes and struggles out
From the throat of the overflowing spout!
Across the windowpane
It pours and pours;
And swift and wide,
With a muddy tide,
Like a river down the gutter roars
The rain, the welcome rain!

Henry Wadsworth Longfellow

MR. FINNEY'S TURNIP

Mr. Finney had a turnip
    And it grew behind the barn;
And it grew and it grew,
    And that turnip did no harm.

There it grew and it grew
    Till it could grow no longer;
Then his daughter Lizzie picked it
    And put it in the cellar.

There it lay and it lay
    Till it began to rot;
And his daughter Susie took it
    And put it in the pot.

And they boiled it and boiled it
    As long as they were able;
And then his daughters took it
    And put it on the table.

Mr. Finney and his wife
    They sat them down to sup;
And they ate and they ate
    And they ate that turnip up.

A SNACK

Three plum buns
    To eat here at the stile
In the clover meadow,
    For we have walked a mile.

One for you, and one for me,
    And one left over.
Give it to the boy who shouts
    To scare sheep from the clover.

Christina Rossetti

THE OLD MAN WITH A BEARD

There was an old man with a beard
Who said, "It is just as I feared!
　　Two owls and a hen,
　　Four larks and a wren,
Have all built their nests in my beard!"

Edward Lear

TWO IN BED

When my brother Tommy
Sleeps in bed with me,
He doubles up
And makes
himself
exactly
like
a
V

And 'cause the bed is not so wide,
A part of him is on my side.

A. B. Ross

ALGY MET A BEAR

Algy met a bear,
The bear was bulgy,
The bulge was Algy.

CLOUDS

White sheep, white sheep,
On a blue hill,
When the wind stops
You all stand still.
When the wind blows
You walk away slow.
White sheep, white sheep,
Where do you go?

Christina Rossetti

OH, FAIR TO SEE

Oh, fair to see
Bloom-laden cherry tree,
  Arrayed in sunny white :
  An April day's delight,
Oh, fair to see!

Oh, fair to see
Fruit-laden cherry tree,
  With balls of shining red
  Decking a leafy head,
Oh, fair to see!

Christina Rossetti

WHEN YOU AND I GROW UP

When you and I
Grow up — Polly —
    I mean that you and me
Shall go sailing in a big ship
    Right over all the sea.
We'll wait till we are older,
    For if we went today,
You know that we might lose ourselves,
    And never find the way.

Kate Greenaway

THE GOLDEN RULE

To do to others as I would
    That they should do to me,
Will make me gentle, kind and good,
    As children ought to be.

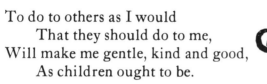

TWENTY FROGGIES

Twenty froggies went to school
Down beside a rushy pool.
Twenty little coats of green,
Twenty vests all white and clean.

"We must be in time," said they,
"First we study, then we play;
That is how we keep the rule,
When we froggies go to school."

Master Bullfrog, brave and stern,
Called his classes in their turn,
Taught them how to nobly strive,
Also how to leap and dive;

Taught them how to dodge a blow,
From the sticks that bad boys throw.
Twenty froggies grew up fast,
Bullfrogs they became at last;

Polished in a high degree,
As each froggie ought to be,
Now they sit on other logs,
Teaching other little frogs.

George Cooper

WINGS

Oh that I had wings like a dove!
For then would I fly away and be at rest.
Lo, then would I wander far off,
And remain in the wilderness.

A Psalm of David

GOOD NIGHT

Baby, baby, lay your head
On your pretty cradle bed;
Shut your eye-peeps, now the day
And the light are gone away;
All the clothes are tuck'd in tight;
Little baby, dear, good night.

Yes, my darling, well I know
How the bitter wind doth blow;
And the winter's snow and rain
Patter on the windowpane;
But they cannot come in here,
To my little baby dear.

For the window shutteth fast,
Till the stormy night is past,
And the curtains warm are spread
Roundabout her cradle bed;
So till morning shineth bright,
Little baby, dear, good night.

Jane Taylor

FROM THE BRIDGE

How silent comes the water round that bend!
Not the minutest whisper does it send
To the o'erhanging willows: blades of grass
Slowly across the checkered shadows pass.

John Keats

THE FUNNY OLD MAN AND HIS WIFE

Once upon a time, in a little wee house,
   Lived a funny old man and his wife;
And he said something funny to make her laugh,
   Every day of his life.

One day he said such a very funny thing,
   That she shook and screamed with laughter;
But the poor old soul, she couldn't leave off
   For at least three whole days after.

So laughing with all her might and main,
   Three days and nights she sat;
And at the end she didn't know a bit
   What she'd been laughing at.

I'M GLAD

I'm glad the sky is painted blue,
    And the earth is painted green,
With such a lot of nice fresh air
    All sandwiched in between.

SCHOOL IS OVER

School is over,
  Oh, what fun!
Lessons finished,
  Play begun.
Who'll run fastest,
  You or I?
Who'll laugh loudest?
  Let us try.

Kate Greenaway

A WEDDING

Rosy apple, lemon and pear,
  Bunch of roses she shall wear,
Gold and silver by her side,
  I know who shall be my bride.

London Street Game

LET DOGS DELIGHT

Let dogs delight to bark and bite,
For God hath made them so.

Isaac Watts

ALL THE BELLS WERE RINGING

All the bells were ringing
And all the birds were singing,
When Molly sat down crying
  For her broken doll:
  O you silly Moll!
Sobbing and sighing
  For a broken doll,
When all the bells are ringing,
And all the birds are singing.

Christina Rossetti

THE FLEA AND THE FLY

A flea and a fly got caught in a flue.
    Said the fly, "Let us flee."
    Said the flea, "Let us fly."
So together they flew through a flaw in the flue.

PEAS

I eat my peas with honey,
I've done it all my life,
They do taste kind of funny,
But it keeps them on the knife.

MR. NOBODY

I know a funny little man,
    As quiet as a mouse,
Who does the mischief that is done
    In everybody's house!
There's no one ever sees his face,
    And yet we all agree
That every plate we break was cracked
    By Mr. Nobody.

'Tis he who always tears our books,
    Who leaves the door ajar,
He pulls the buttons from our shirts,
    And scatters pins afar;
That squeaking door will always squeak,
    For, prithee, don't you see,
We leave the oiling to be done
    By Mr. Nobody.

The fingermarks upon the door
    By none of us are made;
We never leave the blinds unclosed,
    To let the curtains fade.
The ink we never spill; the boots
    That lying round you see
Are not our boots — they all belong
    To Mr. Nobody.

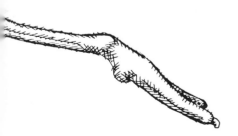

THE OWL

When cats run home and light is come,
And dew is cold upon the ground,
And the far-off stream is dumb,
And the whirring sail goes round;
Alone and warming his five wits,
The white owl in the belfry sits.

When merry milkmaids click the latch,
And rarely smells the new-mown hay,
And the cock hath sung beneath the thatch
Twice or thrice his roundelay;
Alone and warming his five wits,
The white owl in the belfry sits.

Alfred, Lord Tennyson

THE HUMMINGBIRD

The hummingbird, the hummingbird,
So fairy-like and bright;
It lives among the sunny flowers,
A creature of delight.

Mary Howitt

THE OSTRICH IS A SILLY BIRD

The ostrich is a silly bird
With scarcely any mind.
He often runs so very fast,
He leaves himself behind.

And when he gets there, has to stand
And hang about till night,
Without a blessed thing to do
Until he comes in sight.

Mary E. Wilkins Freeman

A SWING SONG

Swing, swing,
Sing, sing,
Here! my throne and I am a king!
Swing, sing,
Swing, sing,
Farewell, earth, for I'm on the wing!

Low, high,
Here I fly,
Like a bird through sunny sky;
Free, free,
Over the lea,
Over the mountain, over the sea!

Up, down,
Up and down,
Which is the way to London Town?
Where? Where?
Up in the air,
Close your eyes and now you are there!

Soon, soon,
Afternoon,
Over the sunset, over the moon;
Far, far,
Over all bar,
Sweeping on from star to star!

No, no,
Low, low,
Sweeping daisies with my toe.
Slow, slow,
To and fro,
Slow — slow — slow — slow.

William Allingham

THE ECHOING GREEN

The sun does arise,
And make happy the skies;
The merry bells ring
To welcome the spring;
The skylark and thrush,
The birds of the bush,
Sing louder around
To the bell's cheerful sound,
While our sports shall be seen
On the echoing green.

Old John with white hair
Does laugh away care,
Sitting under the oak
Among the old folk.
They laugh at our play,
And soon they all say:
"Such, such were the joys
When we, all girls and boys,
In our youth-time were seen
On the echoing green."

Till the little ones, weary,
No more can be merry;
The sun does descend,
And our sports have an end.
Round the laps of their mothers,
Many sisters and brothers,
Like birds in their nest,
Are ready for rest;
And sport no more seen
On the echoing green.

William Blake

WHITE BUTTERFLIES

Fly, white butterflies, out to sea,
Frail, pale wings for the wind to try,
Small white wings that we scarce can see,
    Fly!

Some fly light as a laugh of glee,
Some fly soft as a long, low sigh;
All to the haven where each would be,
    Fly!

Algernon Charles Swinburne

MOTHER

Hundreds of stars in the deep blue sky,
    Hundreds of shells on the shore together,
Hundreds of birds that go singing by,
    Hundreds of birds in the sunny weather.

Hundreds of dewdrops to greet the dawn,
    Hundreds of bees in the purple clover,
Hundreds of butterflies on the lawn,
    But only one mother the wide world over.

George Cooper

TO MY VALENTINE

If apples were pears,
And peaches were plums,
And the rose had a different name —
If tigers were bears,
And fingers were thumbs,
I'd love you just the same!

BABY SEEDS

In a milkweed cradle,
    Snug and warm,
Baby seeds are hiding,
    Safe from harm.
Open wide the cradle,
    Hold it high!
Come, Mr. Wind,
    Help them fly.

GAELIC LULLABY

Hush! the waves are rolling in,
    White with foam, white with foam;
Father toils amid the din;
    But baby sleeps at home.

Hush! the winds roar hoarse and deep —
    On they come, on they come.
Brother seeks the wandering sheep;
    But baby sleeps at home.

Hush! the rain sweeps o'er the knolls,
    Where they roam, where they roam;
Sister goes to seek the cows;
    But baby sleeps at home.

ALL THROUGH THE NIGHT

Sleep, my babe, lie still and slumber,
All through the night,
Guardian angels God will lend thee,
All through the night;
Soft, the drowsy hours are creeping,
Hill and vale in slumber steeping,
Mother, dear, her watch is keeping,
All through the night.

GOOD NIGHT

Good night! Good night!
Far flies the light;
But still God's love
Shall flame above,
Making all bright.
Good night! Good night!

Victor Hugo

NOW I LAY ME DOWN

Now I lay me down to sleep,
I pray thee, Lord, my soul to keep;
Thy love go with me all the night,
And wake me with the morning light.

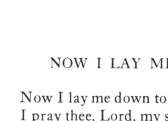

EARLY TO BED

Early to bed and early to rise
Makes a man healthy, wealthy and wise.

Old Proverb

MINNIE AND WINNIE

Minnie and Winnie
    Slept in a shell.
Sleep, little ladies!
    And they slept well.

Pink was the shell within,
    Silver without;
Sounds of the great sea
    Wandered about.

Sleep, little ladies!
    Wake not soon!
Echo on echo
    Dies to the moon.

Two bright stars
    Peeped into the shell.
"What are they dreaming of?
    Who can tell?"

Started a green linnet
    Out of the croft;
Wake, little ladies!
    The sun is aloft.

Alfred, Lord Tennyson

Index of Titles

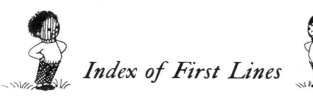

Index of First Lines

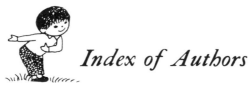

Index of Authors